James

5-Week Women's Bible Study and Prayer Journal

A
beautiful
BIBLE STUDY

Other Bible Studies by Heather Carr

Take Heart: 31-Day Bible Reading Plan and Prayer Journal

James: 5-Week Women's Bible Study and Prayer Journal
© 2018 by Heather Carr

IISBN-13: 978-1986787611

ISBN-10: 1986787613

Requests for information should be addressed to:
Heather@HeatherKernickCarr.com

Table of Contents

A Note from Heather

This journal is designed to go with an online Bible study for women. You'll find free supplementary videos and resources at www.BeautifulBibleStudies.com.

I couldn't believe he'd said that. Talk about humiliating. The seventh grade was hard enough with my gawky limbs and exposed ankles. I had braces, pimples and sure, brushing my curly hair created a frizzy mess. But, that was no excuse to ask me if I'd stuck my finger in a light socket. The nerve of that boy. I was an awkward teenager, to say the least.

Thankfully, I'm no longer stuck in the clumsy transition into physical maturity. In time my body caught up with my arms and legs. I learned to care for my skin and hair. Best of all, I grew comfortable and appreciative of the person God created me to be, blemishes and all.

That in itself is evidence of God's grace if I've ever seen it. Growing up is hard—just ask any middle schooler. Like physical growth, spiritual growth and maturity are a natural progression for followers of Jesus.

Spiritual growth is hard, too. It often strikes when we least expect it in the form of trials or hardships. Our health may fail, our reputation may become tainted or our relationships crumble. We may face financial or emotional insecurity. Lose a loved one. Our world shakes, and we wonder if anything will remain when the trembling subsides.

Our faith is tested and purified in these tough places. If we lean into God and embrace change, we emerge transformed. Our faith is proven authentic. We develop Spirit-led wisdom, compassion and the rare, quiet strength that leads to godly obedience.

James is a book about trial and hope, hard places, and growth. Within the pages of the book of James is a journey toward spiritual transformation and maturity. There is much to be gained from the careful study of this ancient text.

I invite you to join me at as we explore the path to authentic faith and spiritual maturity. If at anytime you'd like to discuss what you're learning, need someone to pray with, or want to proclaim God's goodness, I'd love to hear from you. Join our group of encouraging Christian women at **BeautifulBibleStudies.com**.

Much love,

Heather

How to Use This Journal

1. Gather Your Supplies. You'll need:
- This journal
- A Bible or two (I like to use an NIV Study Bible and an ESV Bible)
- A pen or pencil in whatever colors make you happy
- A blank notebook or journal (if you are reading an electronic copy of this study)

2. The Daily Routine. Over the course of the next 5 weeks, we'll:
- Read daily scripture
- Answer thought-provoking questions about what we've read
- Journal our prayers using the prayer prompts provided
- Explore the context and original language of the text
- Share our journey with a small group or online community
- Rest and reflect on what we've learned

3. Frequently Asked Questions. Just in case you're wondering:
- *What if I fall behind?* No worries. Go at your own pace. If you need a day off or want to spread the daily routine over a couple of days, no problem.
- *How long will this take?* The daily routine can take as little as 10 minutes or as long as an hour or more, depending on your availability and what you hope to gain from your study. There's no right or wrong amount of time, as long as you're spending time with God in his Word.
- *Can I ask you a question?* Yes! Send your question to me at Heather@HeatherKernickCarr.com. I love hearing from you, but I'm a mom to three, so please give me a day or two to get back with you.
- *Will you pray for me?* Yes! Join us at BeautifulBibleStudies.com to submit your prayer request or send me an email. I'm honored to personally pray over each and every request I receive.
- *How do I ask Jesus into my heart?* To ask Jesus into your heart, say this prayer: "Dear God, I know that I've messed up and fallen short of your plan for me. Please forgive me and come into my heart. I trust in Jesus as my savior. Thank you, Lord, for dying on the cross for me. Thank you for forgiving me. Amen." If you've said this prayer for the first time, tell someone like a trusted Christian friend, a pastor or send me a message.

But be doers of the word,

and not hearers only.

James 1:22

CHAPTER

1

Faith in Trials

Read through this week's scripture passage: James chapter 1.

THE BOOK OF JAMES

Theme: Authentic Faith

Author: James, the brother of Jesus

Date: 44 AD – 49 AD

Audience: The Scattered Church of Jerusalem

Overview:

Chapter 1: Faith in Trials
- Authentic faith is proven and strengthened by trials
- Trials produce maturity, endurance and dependence on God
- Trials may lead to temptation
- Temptations are a test of our faith and do not come from God

Chapter 2: Faith in Action
- Authentic faith doesn't show favoritism
- Authentic faith is evident through works
- Faith without works is no faith at all

Chapter 3: Faith Tested
- Authentic faith tames the tongue
- Authentic faith lives by heavenly wisdom

Chapter 4: Willing Faith
- Authentic faith doesn't embrace worldliness
- Authentic faith submits to God's authority and will

Chapter 5: Lasting Faith
- Authentic faith is patient under oppression
- Authentic faith is blessed through prayer and worship
- Authentic faith shows compassion for the lost

PRAYER

Write a prayer thanking God for His word. Ask God to open your heart to receive his word.

Faith in Trials

Read through this week's scripture again, underline any words or phrases that stand out to you.

DID YOU KNOW?

The book of James was originally written in Greek. Because of this, the author's original intent can sometimes be obscured through translation. Consider the following verse:

Consider it pure joy, my brothers and sisters, whenever you face trials of many kinds, because you know that the testing of your faith produces perseverance. Let perseverance finish its work so that you may be mature and complete, not lacking anything. - James 1:2-4 (NIV)

Below you will find some key words from James 1:2-4 along with their Greek counterparts. How does a deeper understanding of the original language enhance your understanding of this key scripture?

trials--Greek peirasmos --"an experiment, attempt, trial, proving "; "a putting to proof"

testing--Greek dokimion --"the proving "; "that by which something is tried or proved, a test "; "to try to learn the genuineness of something by examination and testing"

steadfastness--Greek hypomonē --literally, an abiding under (hupo, "under," menō, "to abide") ; "a patient enduring, sustaining, perseverance"

perfect--Greek teleios--"fully developed"; "denotes that which has reached its maturity"; "wanting nothing necessary to completeness"

plete--holokleros--"complete in all its parts, in no part wanting or unsound, complete, entire, whole"; "complete in every part, i.e. perfectly sound (in body):--entire, whole."

PRAYER

Rewrite the words and phrases you underlined in James Chapter 1 as a prayer back to God.

Faith in Trials

Read James Chapter 1 again. What does this passage tell us about God? Record your observations below.

OBSERVATIONS

PRAYER

Using the list of observations you made, use the space below to offer a prayer of praise to God. Let this prayer be a prayer of praise only, celebrating and thanking God for who He is.

Faith in Trials

Read James Chapter 1 circling any instructions for believers. Write at least one thing you can do today to live out what you've learned.

LIVING THE PROMISE ⟵

....

....

....

....

....

....

....

....

....

....

....

....

....

....

....

....

....

....

....

PRAYER

Use the space below to write a prayer asking God to help you live out His word. If you have any doubts or concerns about your ability, give them over to God in prayer.

THOUGHTS

· ·
· ·
· ·
· ·
· ·
· ·
· ·
· ·
· ·

QUESTIONS

· ·
· ·
· ·
· ·
· ·
· ·
· ·
· ·
· ·

PREPARE
to share

FAVORITES

· ·
· ·
· ·
· ·
· ·
· ·
· ·
· ·
· ·

PRAYER NEEDS

· ·
· ·
· ·
· ·
· ·
· ·
· ·
· ·
· ·

TWO ARE BETTER
than ONE

PRAYER

Write a prayer for your small group, Sunday school class or our online community. Ask that the Lord be honored through your conversation and fellowship time together.

Faith in Trials

Suggested Flow: *Opening Prayer, Read Scripture, Review Prepare to Share Notes, Watch Video, Discuss Questions, Closing Prayer*

1. What is the main idea of the first chapter of the book of James?

2. What do you think James means when he writes, "Count it all joy, my brothers, when you meet trials of various kinds..."?

3. If you find trials difficult to endure, are you committing a sin? Why or why not?

4. What does James say about temptation?

5. What is the relationship between trials, wisdom and temptation?

6 . What does James say about religion?

7. How is pure religion different than worthless religion?

8. How are the ideas of a pure, faultless religion and a worthless religion important to our lives as believers?

REST & REFLECT

A verse to meditate on this week: Let perseverance finish its work so

that you may be mature and complete, not lacking anything.

James 1:4

For as the body apart

from the spirit is dead,

so also *faith* apart

from works is dead.

- James 2:26

CHAPTER

2

Faith in Action

Read through this week's scripture passage: James Chapter 2.

AUTHOR AND DATE

There are four men named James mentioned in the New Testament: James the Less, the son of Alphaeus (Matt. 10:3; Acts 1:13), James the father of Judas, not Iscariot (Luke 6:16, Acts 1:13), James the son of Zebedee and brother of John, (Matt. 4:21), and James the brother of Jesus and brother of Jude, who wrote the book of Jude (Mark 6:3, Matt. 13:55). James the Less and James the father of Judas weren't considered serious contenders as possible authors for this letter. James the son of Zebedee was martyred in 44 A.D. (Acts 12:2), leaving James the brother of Jesus as the most likely author of the book of James.

Other evidence supports this theory. Another letter from James the brother of Jesus is recorded in Acts 15. These two letters are similar in style and format. The letter is written with the authority of one who has seen the resurrected Jesus (1 Cor. 15:7), was an associate of the apostles (Gal. 1:19), and was an established leader of the church (Acts 12:17; 15:13; 21:18; Gal. 2:12).

James was called one of the "pillars" of the Jerusalem church along with Peter and John (Gal. 2:9). Initially, James rejected Jesus as the Messiah (John 7:5), but he later believed (1 Cor. 15:7). He was so deeply devoted to righteousness that he became known as "James the Just." The first century Jewish historian Josephus recorded James' death by the sword as occurring ca. 62 AD.

James likely wrote this letter to the believers who left Jerusalem as a result of the persecution recorded in Acts 12 (ca. 44 AD). Since there is no mention of the Council of Jerusalem that is described in Acts 15 (ca. 49 AD), James is dated by many as written between 44 – 49 AD, though some date it as late as 62 AD, the year of James' martyrdom.

PRAYER

Write a prayer thanking God for His word. Ask God to open your heart to receive his word.

Faith in Action

Read through this week's scripture again, underline any words or phrases that stand out to you.

YOU SEE THAT HIS FAITH AND HIS ACTIONS WERE WORKING TOGETHER, AND HIS FAITH WAS MADE COMPLETE BY WHAT HE DID. - JAMES 2:22 NIV

Working Together—Greek *synergeō*— to be a fellow-worker, i.e. co-operate:—help (work) with, work(-er) together.

Actions—Greek *ergon*—toil (as an effort or occupation); by implication, an act:—deed, doing, labor, work.

Made Complete—Greek *teleioō*— to complete, i.e. (literally) accomplish, or (figuratively) consummate (in character):—consecrate, finish, fulfill, make perfect.

PRAYER

Rewrite the words and phrases you underlined in James Chapter 2 as a prayer back to God.

Faith in Action

Read James Chapter 2 again. What does this passage tell us about God? Record your observations below.

OBSERVATIONS

PRAYER

Using the list of observations you made, use the space below to offer a prayer of praise to God. Let this prayer be a prayer of praise only, celebrating and thanking God for who He is.

Faith in Action

Read James Chapter 2 circling any instructions for believers. Write at least one thing you can do today to live out what you've learned.

LIVING THE PROMISE ⇐

....

....

....

....

....

....

....

....

....

....

....

....

....

....

....

....

....

....

....

....

PRAYER

Use the space below to write a prayer asking God to help you live out His word. If you have any doubts or concerns about your ability, give them over to God in prayer.

THOUGHTS

. . . .
. . . .
. . . .
. . . .
. . . .
. . . .
. . . .
. . . .
. . . .
. . . .
. . . .

QUESTIONS

. . . .
. . . .
. . . .
. . . .
. . . .
. . . .
. . . .
. . . .
. . . .
. . . .
. . . .

PREPARE to share

FAVORITES

. . . .
. . . .
. . . .
. . . .
. . . .
. . . .
. . . .
. . . .
. . . .
. . . .
. . . .

THOUGHTS

PRAYER NEEDS

. . . .
. . . .
. . . .
. . . .
. . . .
. . . .
. . . .
. . . .
. . . .
. . . .
. . . .

TWO ARE BETTER than ONE

PRAYER

Write a prayer for your small group, Sunday school class or our online community. Ask that the Lord be honored through your conversation and fellowship time together.

Faith in Action

Suggested Flow: Opening Prayer, Read Scripture, Review Prepare to Share Notes, Watch Video, Discuss Questions, Closing Prayer

1. In your opinion, what is the most important verse in James Chapter 2? Why?

2. What does James say about favoritism?

3. What does James mean when he writes, "Speak and act as those who are going to be judged by the law that gives freedom..."?

4. How is the idea of mercy triumphing over judgment important to believers today?

5. What do you think James means when he says, "Show me your faith without deeds, and I will show you my faith by my deeds."?

6 . James writes that Abraham's faith was completed by his works. How does this relate to last week's meditation, "Let perseverance finish its work so that you may be mature and complete, not lacking anything."(James 1:4)?

7. How would you respond to someone who said being concerned about our actions as Christians is the same as following a false 'works-based' Christianity?

8. How does the law bring freedom to our lives today?

REST&REFLECT

A verse to meditate on this week: What good is it, my brothers, if someone says he has faith but does not have works? Can that faith save him? - James 2:14

Day Seven

But the wisdom from above is first pure, then
peaceable, gentle, open to reason, full of mercy
and good fruits, impartial and sincere.

- James 3:17 -

CHAPTER

3

Faith Tested

Read Romans 3:27-4:5

On the surface, Paul's instructions to the Roman church seem to be in contradiction with James' teaching in Chapter 2. Since we know the word of God doesn't contradict itself, how is this possible?

To understand, let's take a look at another letter Paul wrote. In Galatians 5:6 Paul writes, "For in Christ Jesus neither circumcision nor uncircumcision counts for anything, but only faith working through love." In other words, it's not works like circumcision that win God's favor. It's faith working through love.

Faith makes us righteous in God's eyes through Jesus' sacrifice for us. Faith naturally works through love. Faith produces love for God. Love for God produces obedience to God. And, obedience to God produces loving works. This is the living faith James is writing about.

Both James and Paul point toward Abraham as an example. Abraham's faith makes him righteous in God's eyes (Gen. 15:6). His willingness to sacrifice Isaac in obedience to God proves his faith is alive.

Essentially, these teachings correct two different false beliefs. Paul is refuting the idea that you can win God over by doing all the "right" things. In reality, the only way to be justified in God's sight is through faith in Jesus. Jesus taught this when he said, "I am the way, and the truth, and the life. No one comes to the Father except through me" (John 14:6). James is dismissing the belief that you can be a loveless person, go on sinning and living selfishly because faith will get you into heaven. This isn't what Jesus teaches, just take a look at the Parable of the Good Samaritan in Luke 10. Compassion requires action.

When Paul teaches in Romans 4:5 that we are justified by faith alone, he means we can only be made right with God through faith in Jesus. When James says in James 2:24 that we are not justified by faith alone he means that living faith leads to love for and obedience to God, which naturally lead to loving works. These ideas don't contradict one another, they support the teaching of Jesus.

PRAYER

Write a prayer thanking God for his Word. Ask God to open your heart to receive the Word.

Faith Tested

Read through this week's scripture again, underline any words or phrases that stand out to you.

PEACEMAKERS WHO SOW IN PEACE REAP A HARVEST OF RIGHTEOUSNESS. - JAMES 3:18 (NIV)

Righteousness—Greek *dikaiosynē*—state of him who is as he ought to be, righteousness, the condition acceptable to God; integrity, virtue, purity of life, rightness, correctness of thinking feeling, and acting

Peace—Greek *eirēnē*—peace between individuals, i.e. harmony, concord; the tranquil state of a soul assured of its salvation through Christ, and so fearing nothing from God and content with its earthly lot, of whatsoever sort that is

Make, reap—Greek *poieō*—to produce, bear, shoot forth; to be the authors of a thing (to cause, bring about)

PRAYER

Rewrite the words and phrases you underlined in James Chapter 3 as a prayer back to God.

Faith Tested

Read James Chapter 3 again. What does this passage tell us about God? Record your observations below.

OBSERVATIONS

PRAYER

Using the list of observations you made, use the space below to offer a prayer of praise to God. Let this prayer be a prayer of praise only, celebrating and thanking God for who He is.

Faith Tested

Read James Chapter 3 circling any instructions for believers. Write at least one thing you can do today to live out what you've learned.

LIVING THE PROMISE ←

....

....

....

....

....

....

....

....

....

....

....

....

....

....

....

....

....

....

....

....

PRAYER

Use the space below to write a prayer asking God to help you live out His word. If you have any doubts or concerns about your ability, give them over to God in prayer.

THOUGHTS

....
....
....
....
....
....
....
....

PREPARE
to *share*

QUESTIONS

....
....
....
....
....
....
....
....

FAVORITES

....
....
....
....
....
....
....
....

PRAYER NEEDS

....
....
....
....
....
....
....
....

TWO ARE BETTER than ONE

PRAYER

Write a prayer for your small group, Sunday school class or our online community. Ask that the Lord be honored through your conversation and fellowship time together.

Faith Tested

Suggested Flow: Opening Prayer, Read Scripture, Review Prepare to Share Notes, Watch Video, Discuss Questions, Closing Prayer

1. What is James asking us to do in Chapter 3?

2. How does James describe the tongue?

3. What is the problem with speaking positive, encouraging words in one situation, then speaking negative, critical words in another?

4. Why should Christians care about the words we speak?

5. What is the difference between earthly wisdom and heavenly wisdom?

6 . Why do you think James returns to the idea of wisdom after warning us of the dangers of the tongue?

7. How do you determine whether advice you receive is rooted in heavenly or earthly wisdom?

8. What do you think James means when he writes, "Peacemakers who sow in peace reap a harvest of righteousness."?

REST & REFLECT

A verse to meditate on this week: And a harvest of righteousness is sown in peace by those who make peace. - James 3:18

Submit yourselves therefore to God.
Resist the devil, and he will flee from you.

- James 4:7 -

CHAPTER

4

Read through this week's scripture passage: James Chapter 4.

FURTHER READING: A COLLECTION OF CROSS-REFERENCES

Have you ever noticed how so many passages of scripture support and agree with one another? Considering that the Bible is a collection of 66 different books, that's pretty amazing. Add in that it was written by 40 different authors on three different continents over the course of about 2,000 years and well, I'd say that's miraculous.

Our study of James doesn't have to end with his written words. We can verify and strengthen our understanding by reading what other authors in the Bible have to say on the same topics.

Here are some scriptures to explore as you study James Chapter 4:

Genesis 8:21 • Job 14:1-2 • Psalm 63:1-11 • Psalm 68:21 • Psalm 75:6 • Psalm 84:2 • Psalm 89:47 • Psalm 101:5 • Psalm 110:1-2 • Psalm 140:11 • Psalm 143:6 • Proverbs 16:28 • Proverbs 17:9 • Proverbs 26:20 • Isaiah 6:5 • Isaiah 66:2 • Jeremiah 3:1, 6, 8-9 • Hosea 4:15 • Matthew 5:4 • Matthew 10:38 • Matthew 22:37 • Matthew 23:12 • Mark 14:72 • Luke 12:13-21 • Acts 21:14 • Romans 7:5, 23 • Romans 8:5-7 • Romans 15:32 • 1 Corinthians 1:10 • 1 Corinthians 16:7 • 2 Corinthians 6:14-18 • Titus 2:11-12 • Titus 3:2 • Hebrews 7:19 • Hebrews 10:22 • 1 Peter 5:5 • 2 Peter 3:9 • Jude 18

Day One

PRAYER

Write a prayer thanking God for His word. Ask God to open your heart to receive his word.

Read through this week's scripture again, underline any words or phrases that stand out to you.

SUBMIT YOURSELVES, THEN, TO GOD. RESIST THE DEVIL, AND HE WILL FLEE FROM YOU.
- JAMES 4:7 (NIV)

Submit—Greek *hypotassō*—to subordinate; reflexively, to obey:—be under obedience (obedient), put under, subdue unto, (be, make) subject (to, unto), be (put) in subjection (to, under), submit self unto.

Resist—Greek *anthistēmi*—to stand against, i.e. oppose:—resist, withstand.

He will flee—Greek *pheugō*—to run away (literally or figuratively); by implication, to shun; by analogy, to vanish:—escape, flee (away).

PRAYER

Rewrite the words and phrases you underlined in James Chapter 4 as a prayer back to God.

Willing Faith

Read James Chapter 4 again. What does this passage tell us about God? Record your observations below.

OBSERVATIONS

PRAYER

Using the list of observations you made, use the space below to offer a prayer of praise to God. Let this prayer be a prayer of praise only, celebrating and thanking God for who He is.

Willing Faith

Read James Chapter 4 circling any instructions for believers. Write at least one thing you can do today to live out what you've learned.

LIVING THE PROMISE ⇐

....

....

....

....

....

....

....

....

....

....

....

....

....

....

....

....

....

....

....

PRAYER

Use the space below to write a prayer asking God to help you live out His word. If you have any doubts or concerns about your ability, give them over to God in prayer.

THOUGHTS

· ·
· ·
· ·
· ·
· ·
· ·
· ·
· ·
· ·
· ·

QUESTIONS

· ·
· ·
· ·
· ·
· ·
· ·
· ·
· ·
· ·
· ·

PREPARE to share

FAVORITES

· ·
· ·
· ·
· ·
· ·
· ·
· ·
· ·
· ·
· ·

THOUGHTS

PRAYER NEEDS

· ·
· ·
· ·
· ·
· ·
· ·
· ·
· ·
· ·
· ·

QUESTIONS

TWO ARE BETTER than ONE

PRAYER

Write a prayer for your small group, Sunday school class or our online community. Ask that the Lord be honored through your conversation and fellowship time together.

Willing Faith

Suggested Flow: *Opening Prayer, Read Scripture, Review Prepare to Share Notes, Watch Video, Discuss Questions, Closing Prayer.*

1. What do you think is the most important verse in James Chapter 4? Why?

2. What does James say about the source of fighting among people?

3. How does the act of submitting to God impact our relationships with others?

4. How do you personally handle disagreements with other Christians? With those who don't yet know the Lord?

5. What advice does James give to those tempted by the world?

6 . How is speaking against one another connected to the law?

7. Why should we be careful about the plans we make?

8. How do you include God's will in your plans for the future?

REST & REFLECT

A verse to meditate on this week: Draw near to God, and he will draw near to you. - James 4:8

The prayer of a righteous person is
powerful and effective.

- James 5:16 -

CHAPTER

5

Lasting Faith

Read through this week's scripture passage: James Chapter 5.

Is anyone among you sick? Let them call the elders of the church to pray over them and anoint them with oil in the name of the Lord. And the prayer offered in faith will make the sick person well; the Lord will raise them up. If they have sinned, they will be forgiven. - James 5:13-15 (NIV)

Three days in the hospital and my doctors still didn't understand what was wrong, let alone how to heal me. I did everything I knew to do: gave up the foods I loved, exercised, followed my doctor's orders to the letter, even underwent surgery. My church prayed over me and anointed me more than once. I felt certain God was going to heal me. Yet there I was, wondering why?

This scripture says God will heal, so how come sometimes He doesn't? In Mark 2, Jesus explains why He's going to heal the paralytic man when He says, "I am doing this so you may know the Son of Man has power on earth to forgive sins."

Jesus is able to heal us, but His primary concern is our spiritual well-being. Paul encountered this too, he writes, "The things God showed me were so great. But to keep me from being too full of pride because of seeing these things, I have been given trouble in my body." (2 Cor. 12:7-10 NLT)

Paul was a man of faith who asked for healing, but it didn't happen. I still live with chronic illness and more questions than answers when it comes to my health. By the grace of God with the help of a team of specialists, I've learned to manage my symptoms.

We are called to pray, anoint the sick, and to believe God is able to heal. It's not our lack of faith that keeps us or our loved ones from being restored to good health. It's living in a fallen world, and God's desire to do what's best for us, even when we don't understand.

PRAYER

Write a prayer thanking God for His word. Ask God to open your heart to receive his word.

Lasting Faith

° • °

Read through this week's scripture again, underline any words or phrases that stand out to you.

IS ANYONE AMONG YOU SICK? LET THEM CALL THE ELDERS OF THE CHURCH TO PRAY OVER THEM AND ANOINT THEM WITH OIL IN THE NAME OF THE LORD. AND THE PRAYER OFFERED IN FAITH WILL MAKE THE SICK PERSON WELL; THE LORD WILL RAISE THEM UP. IF THEY HAVE SINNED, THEY WILL BE FORGIVEN. - JAMES 5:14-15 (NIV)

Sick—Greek *astheneō*—to be feeble (in any sense):—be diseased, impotent folk (man), (be) sick, (be, be made) weak.

Will make well—Greek *sōzō*—to save, i.e. deliver or protect (literally or figuratively):—heal, preserve, save (self), do well, be (make) whole.

Forgiven—Greek *aphiēmi*— to send forth, in various applications (as follow):—cry, forgive, forsake, lay aside, leave, let (alone, be, go, have), omit, put (send) away, remit, suffer, yield up.

PRAYER

Rewrite the words and phrases you underlined in James Chapter 5 as a prayer back to God.

Lasting Faith

Read James Chapter 5 again. What does this passage tell us about God? Record your observations below.

OBSERVATIONS

PRAYER

Using the list of observations you made, use the space below to offer a prayer of praise to God. Let this prayer be a prayer of praise only, celebrating and thanking God for who He is.

Lasting Faith

Read James Chapter 5 circling any instructions for believers. Write at least one thing you can do today to live out what you've learned.

LIVING THE PROMISE ⇐

....

....

....

....

....

....

....

....

....

....

....

....

....

....

....

....

....

....

....

PRAYER

Use the space below to write a prayer asking God to help you live out His word. If you have any doubts or concerns about your ability, give them over to God in prayer.

THOUGHTS

....
....
....
....
....
....
....
....
....
....
....
....

PREPARE
to *share*

QUESTIONS

....
....
....
....
....
....
....
....
....
....
....
....

FAVORITES

....
....
....
....
....
....
....
....
....
....
....
....

TWO ARE BETTER *than* ONE

PRAYER NEEDS

....
....
....
....
....
....
....
....
....
....
....
....

PRAYER

Write a prayer for your small group, Sunday school class or our online community. Ask that the Lord be honored through your conversation and fellowship time together.

Lasting Faith

Suggested Flow: Opening Prayer, Read Scripture, Review Prepare to Share Notes, Watch Video, Discuss Questions, Closing Prayer

1. If you could summarize this chapter in one word or phrase, what would you choose? Why?

2. What can we learn from James' warning to the rich?

3. Is wealth in and of itself a sin? Why or why not?

4. According to James, what does it mean to be patient in times of oppression?

5. How do Christians in your church or community face oppression today?

6 . What does James say about the importance of prayer and confession?

7. What do you think it means to turn a sinner from the error of their way?

8. What changes could you make to improve your current prayer life?

REST & REFLECT

A verse to meditate on this week: Is anyone among you suffering?

Let him pray. Is anyone cheerful? Let him sing praise. - James 5:13

Day Seven

Thank You

Before you go, I'd like to say thank you for taking this journey through the book of James with me. I know your time is valuable and there are many Bible study resources available to you. I am both honored and humbled that you chose to spend your most valuable time of the day with one of my resources.

If you enjoyed this Bible Study and Prayer Journal, I could really use your help. Please take a minute to write a review on Amazon or recommend this study to a friend. Your feedback and encouragement help me create Bible study resources that encourage your spiritual growth and intimate relationship with God.

For more free Bible study resources please visit my online women's Bible study community at BeautifulBibleStudies.com.

Made in the USA
Middletown, DE
26 February 2024

50386605R00051